12-15-06

Laugh and
Live Happier:

P.L.A.Y.S. For Life

Jana Ruth

B.A., M.S., C.L.L,
A.D.D., S.U.P.,
X.Y.Z, P.O.Q.,
H.A., H.A., H.O.,
T.E.E., H.E.E.

Copyright @ 2006

All rights reserved

One Woman's Laughter Press
Tempe, Arizona 85282

Printed in the USA

First Printing: November 2006
Second Printing: December 2006

ISBN 1-59916-115-X

1. Humor   2. Self-help

480-897-7269 (Phone)
j.ruth@cox.net
www.janaruth.biz

To my Mom and Dad
Betty and Mayland Parker
For allowing, encouraging, and
helping me
Laugh!

This Is The Key

This is the key of the kingdom:
In that kingdom there is a city.
In that city there is a town.
In that town there is a street.
In that street there is a lane.
In that lane there is a yard.
In that yard there is a house.
In that house there is a room.
In that room there is a bed.
On that bed there is a basket.
In that basket there are some flowers.
Flowers in the basket.
Basket on the bed.
Bed in the room.
Room in the house.
House in the yard.
Yard in the lane.
Lane in the street
Street in the town.
Town in the city.
City in the kingdom.
Of the kingdom, this is the key.

Anonymous

Contents

A BIG WARNING

WARNING: You may want to stop reading _now_ before you start because I can't guarantee what will happen to you if you continue to read this book. I refuse to take responsibility. Some people that take themselves WAY, did I say, WAY, too seriously, start to enjoy life, and it can sometimes cause them to have some serious side effects. Some of the side affects include laughing for no reason, smiling like an idiot, and one really bad thing, they start to smile at people they know, and even worse, people they don't know and they can't say why they do it. So if any of these things happen, I am sorry but you can't have your money back, and you will have to figure out how to explain your new positive attitude to your family and friends. Don't say I didn't warn you, because not only did I warn you, but also I warned you in CAPITAL LETTERS. End of WARNING

PLAY 07007

The Structure...

It is belief in roses that bring them to bloom.
French Proverb

This book is divided into two parts. The first part of the book is the story of how I came to write this book. It tells what and who influenced me to get to the place where I am today.

Before we go further I must put in a disclaimer: *All persons and events depicted in Part 1 are totally biased and true based on my memory. Remember I used drugs in the 1960's, and unlike President Clinton I did inhale.*

The second part of the book is about the P.L.A.Y.S. acronym and how to use it as a Playbook for a happier life.

So if you just want to get to the main part of the book, go now to the second part. I won't feel bad or even know. To be honest, I wrote the first part for me and a few family members and close friends anyway. It makes the book that much longer and I can charge more money. So do whatever feels right for you. I am okay with this idea; I hope that you are okay with it too.

In Part 2 of this Playbook and at the end of each of the PLAYS of the acronym P.L.A.Y.S. is a blank sheet for you to PLAY with and it can be used for anything you want. My suggestion would be to use it for reflection and ideas you can use from that PLAY. To jumpstart your creativity, instead of using words or letters on that page, draw out the main concepts and ideas using pictures and symbols that you got from that Play. Anyway, as it states, it is <u>Your Page To Play With</u>.

So just have fun and laugh a little and PLEASE DON'T TAKE THIS BOOK TOO SERIOUSLY!

PLAY 1257

The Reason...

One joy scatters a hundred griefs.
Chinese Proverb

About 15 to 20 years ago, because of personal experience I decided to offer a workshop, I mean <u>playshop</u>, (you have to admit that sounds more fun), to employees called Humor and Laughter in the Workplace (maybe we should change Workplace to Playplace?). There was much research that had been done and continues to be done that proves that the more fun, play, and laughter that there is in the workplace (playplace), the more productive people will be.

So, because of my experience in theater and my love of laughter and play, I decided to take my knowledge and experience and help others to laugh and live happier. Those playshops and what I learned and continue to learn from them are the reason for this book. My hope is that you view this book as a Playbook for a happier life.

Part 1

She Looks Like a Bird!

PLAY 12

In the Beginning...

He/she who laughs; lasts.
Unknown

In the beginning there was laughter and I was born at a very young age and already my life was a joke. 'Joke' in Webster's Dictionary has many meanings but the one that fits my life is the one that says, "a joke is something not to be taken seriously." I have never taken my life seriously, even from the beginning. You see, I was only 4 pounds 12 ounces at birth, and everyone, mostly my family and my friends, laughed at me. I looked like a bird, and a scrawny bird at that. The doctors should have treated me as a premature baby, but they wanted to see if I could live without that treatment.

I come from mixed parents, one mother and one father. I was so surprised at my birth that I didn't speak for a year and a half. Right at the beginning I got the joke gene, "don't take your life too seriously." I realized that my life was a joke and a warning for other people. I smiled and laughed all the time, even though I was a sickly baby. When I was about a year old my parents took me to the hospital because I was very sick, the nurse looked at me and said "she doesn't look sick." I smiled and threw-up all over the nurse...and then really laughed. My life is a joke, and that's how I want it. I don't want to take my life or myself too seriously.

PLAY 92965423

The Childhood...

Sometimes a laugh is the only weapon we have.
Roger Rabbit

When I was ten I had an experience in how wonderful and powerful the sound of laughter could be. I was doing a skit in church and ad-lipped (another early discovery), and discovered the glorious rich sound of laughter that I had created. Hooked I was. Right then and there I decided that I must find ways to help myself and other people laugh. I had discovered my passion, which many people spend their entire lives looking for and I was lucky enough to discover mine at age 10.

Soon after this wonderful, life-changing experience, I discovered the major role model of my life, Carol Burnett. She was on the old "Garry Moore Show," and I made my younger bother play Derwood Kirby and we would act out all their skits. I loved and still love Carol Burnett. She was and is a very funny woman. She made me laugh, and I loved her strength, her intelligence, and her Tarzan Call was something to die for.

When Carol Burnett got her own show many years later, I was very jealous of Vicki Lawrence who was chosen to play Carol's younger sister, Chrissie, on the show. This character was based on Carol Burnett's real younger sister; I thought Vicki would never last. I really believed that somehow they would discover me and ditch Vicki. Of course I was only 17 or 18 at the time and didn't have even close to Vicki's talent, but that didn't matter to me. I was sure that Carol, or other people on her show, would realize that hiring Vicki was a mistake and somehow they would discover me and replace Vickie with me. As I am sure, you realize it never happened. I always thought it was the show's loss that they didn't discover me.

PLAY 0970

The College Experience...

Forget injuries, never forget kindnesses.
Confucius

When I got to college at Arizona State University, I majored in Speech and Theater. I had gotten the acting bug after seeing and falling in love with Carol Burnett and all the other comedians of that time: Red Shelton, Johnny Carson, and Lucille Ball. I loved to laugh, and even though I was still painfully shy while in high school, I found, with acting, that I could stop being shy and insecure and become a different person, and that was exciting.

The Bra Date

During college I discovered something about myself, I loved to play, laugh, and be involved in practical jokes; I started doing these things on a much more conscious basis. While in high school, a couple of my friends and I discovered a clothing shop in Scottsdale, Arizona that had bras of different sizes in their display window. The sizes of the bras went from the training bra, (Why do we call it a training bra? What are we training? The nipples? The breasts? If we have a training bra, why don't we have a training jock? After all, the penis seems to be in as great or greater need for training!) all the way up to 58DD. We asked what size the biggest bra was. As soon as we found out there was a bra that size for sale, we threatened to buy it for each other. Of the three of us, I was without, a doubt the one that needed it the least. I was closer to the training bra than the 58DD. I never followed through on my threat, but my friends did.

The Christmas of my Freshman (Freshwoman) year, my friends presented me with a 52DD. The saleswoman would not sell them the 58DD; she only had one 58DD bra and wanted to keep it for someone who really needed it.

My friends had starched the bra and as I opened up the present, one cup was sticking up looking at me. My family, who all had and have great senses of humor, insisted that I put the bra on and model it, so with the help of a couple of pillows, I put the bra over my clothes and modeled it...to the delight of my family.

So now what to do with the bra? I decided that since I lived on campus in a dorm, and on the 5th floor of the dorm facing the street, I would use my bra as a flag. Each morning I would hang the bra out the window. That was before they stopped making buildings with windows, and each night I would pull the bra back in. My roommate at the time thought it was kind of strange, but also funny, besides she had been one of the girls who gave me the bra.

One day when I was in my room studying, I heard a male voice yelling up at me, he said, "Hey, girl, with the big bra. Girl, with the big bra, if you are there I would like to talk to you." Well, I walked over to the window, and in my best Mae West voice said, "Hey, there big boy, why don't you come up and see me some time, maybe right now?" He answered, "I don't want to talk to you I want to talk to the girl who fits that bra." I answered, still doing Mae West, "Big Boy, that's me. I fit the big bra." "Okay," he said, somewhat disappointed, "come down I would like to meet you." So, I went downstairs, and met Tom, and we started dating. I think we both admired the courage of each other. He admired me putting the bra out in the first place and I admired his courage in asking to meet me.

So after dating for two to three months, he suggested that I wear the bra, stuffed and under my clothes, on a date with him, and he would wear glasses without any lens and keep rubbing his eyes. I guess he don't think the bra was funny enough or maybe he just wanted to join in on the fun, but there he was with his lens less glasses when he picked me up for the date.

It took me several hours to get the bra to look somewhat normal and I had to borrow many pairs of socks and nylons to stuff the bra. Luckily it was wintertime and I wore a coat, otherwise I think I might have fallen over since I had so much weight going forward. At the time I was 5' 7" and only weighed 115 pounds.

As Tom did not have a car we needed to
walk to the restaurant and set out on our
adventure. We had laughed for about half
a mile and then calmed down enough to be
talking about other things besides my bra.
While walking down Rural Road, in Tempe,
Arizona, we heard the screeching brakes
of a car. We turned around and four
males were sitting in a car goggled-eyed
with mouths open and all fixated on my
chest. I turned and waved, and Tom and
I set out walking again.

We finally got to the restaurant and we
had decided that Tom was going to ask
for an intimate table and we were going
to hold hands across the table. Before
that happened as we walked into the
restaurant we could tell immediately that
we were the center of attention. The
restaurant was very crowded which made
it even more fun. The reactions to us
varied. Some people starred at us from
the time we walked into the restaurant
until they left or we left. Some people
would look at me and quickly look away.
Some people refused to even look. I must
have been a sight to see. I was very thin,
with an enormous chest. It is important to

remember this was before breast implants and Dolly Parton. People were not used to seeing women with such big breasts.

The hostess came up to us and she was about 5' 3", about my chest level, and she could not take her eyes off my breasts and said, "How many?" I in my Mae West voice said, "Two honey. Two. Just two." The hostess's eyes got even bigger and her mouth was so open, a truck could have driven through and she wouldn't have noticed. Tom said, "We want the smallest table you got. It's our honeymoon, and we are really in love." The whole time he is talking to her he is rubbing his left eye with his finger through the hole where the lens should have been.

I don't know how either one of us didn't start laughing; I think acting was helping me out. Tom, I don't know because I think he was majoring in Business. Maybe they teach acting in Business (because there sure has been a lot of acting going on in Enron and some other companies of late). Anyway, the hostess showed us to our table and it was a small table. So Tom and I played like very passionate lovers and held hands across the table.

With such large breasts and sitting so close to the table, I found that my breasts pretty much covered the table. It wasn't a problem until the waitress came to deliver our food, and than it was a major problem. There was no place to put the food. She walked to my side, and my breasts had that side covered, she than walked to Tom's side and it was covered. We did want to eat so we decided that we needed to stop holding hands. Once I let his hands go, there was room on his side of the table for both our dinners. So I ate that night reaching over the table and eating my dinner on his side of the table.

For the rest of the evening and the walk home there was no other incident. We had planned though, one more practical joke that we wanted to play on the dorm mother. Each dorm had a dorm mother, who sat at the entrance of the dorm to make sure the proper people were coming into the dorm.

My dorm mother was this little old woman, probably younger than me now (55) who took herself and her job very seriously. I have always found people who take themselves too seriously a challenge, and want to do something to get them out of their seriousness.

So we had decided to go back to Tom's dorm, which was right next to mine and remove my bra, socks, nylons, and all. Tom put the bra under his coat and I had the socks and nylons in a paper bag. We went to my dorm and kissed good night. I started to walk past the dorm mother on the way to my room, when Tom pulled out the bra, and said, "Jana, you have forgotten this." "Oh", I said, pretending to be embarrassed, and ran back to grab the bra out of Tom's hand. "Thank you," I said, as I ran past the dorm mother again and up the stairs. The look on her face was priceless.

For the next couple of weeks whenever she saw me, she said, "I think you must have a good time with your boyfriend," and then she would wink at me. I think she saw our stunt, as just that, a stunt, and I don't think she took herself as seriously as I had thought. As a dorm mother, like all mothers, I am sure she had experienced many things, and was wise beyond years.

The Siamese Twin Double Date

One other college experience that I will share to show how I was discovering the power of laughter and play was my Siamese twin double date. My roommate, Janet, and her boyfriend, Danny, and our other friend Marilyn and I were all sitting in the library attempting to study but really talking. Danny asked Marilyn and me which one of us would like to go on a blind date with his friend Ray on Friday night. He said it would be a double date because he and Janet would come along with us. Both Marilyn and I stated our extreme dislike to blind dates. They never worked out, and were almost always painful and embarrassing.

We said we would both pass. Sorry, but it wasn't going to happen for either one of us. I said, "If both Marilyn and I could go then I might consider it, but since we both can't go, just forget it."

"Wait, a minute, wait a minute that is a great idea. You can both go."

These were Danny's words. Danny, for 19, looked 30 and acted about 12. He was like a little imp. He was about 5' 5" and about 170 pounds. He looked like a young Santa Claus without the beard and red clothes.

"Wait a minute yourself," both Marilyn and I said together. "We can't both go," "Oh, yes you can," Danny said. "You can go as Siamese twins." Now Marilyn and I looked nothing alike. I weighted 115 and had a long thin face; she weighed about 150 and had a short fat face. I had long straight hair and she had short curly hair. We were as far apart from any kind of twins, let alone Siamese twins as you could get. The only things we had in common was the same hair color, brown, and were the same height, 5' 7". We really knew nothing about Siamese twins, as I still don't. The only thing we knew was that somehow they were attached.

"How are we going to be attached?" Marilyn asked Danny. "That's easy," he said "we will attach your legs, one leg each, and we will attach them from the top of your knee to your waist." He had us standing up side by side to see if it would work. "Come on, you guys, it will be fun." Danny giggled. Janet, who hadn't said anything said, "I think you should do it. It will be such a trip!" "Trip" was one of those words we used in the 1970's, along with "groovy" and "far out."

So Marilyn looked at me and I looked at Marilyn and she said, "I will do it if you will," I said, "Yes, let's do it." So Danny told Ray that he had a date with Jana Marilyn Cruise. We put our names together. Ray thought he had one date with one girl. Boy, was he in for a surprise.

I have often wondered about Ray and if the experience with us on the blind date messed him up for life. It is amazing sometimes to think about people who come into your life just briefly and what a difference they make, or what great stories they give you. Ray was one of those people.

The afternoon of the big date came and Marilyn came over to Janet and my dorm room at around 4:00 p.m. We wanted time to practice. We were going to the rodeo around 7:00 p.m. We decided to wear matching jeans and sew one leg from my jeans with one leg from her jeans. Luckily Marilyn was a great seamstress and sewed the jeans with thick and strong thread that could not be seen. So Marilyn sewed up the jeans and to put them on we had to lie down side by side on the floor and slowly pull the jeans up at the same time. Well, we got laughing so hard that we pulled the seams out of the jeans. So Marilyn sewed them up again and back on the floor we went as we pulled the jeans up again. This time they stayed, and now Marilyn and I needed to practice. We had to coordinate walking, and to decide which foot to start walking with.

So for the next hour and a half we practiced. Janet coached us on how to walk and move as we walked up and down the floors of the dorm. We practiced going up and down steps because we knew we had to go down three steps to get to the lobby where Ray, Janet, and Danny would be waiting for us. Girls would meet us in the halls and ask us what we were doing, and they would laugh and ask what time is he coming; they wanted to be there to witness this. I don't think there are many girls we have had a good experience on a blind date.

Finally at 7:15 pm, (Ray was late,) we made our way to the lobby where Ray and Danny were waiting for us. Janet went ahead of us to be with Danny and Ray and watch our grand entrance. After all this time we were sick of each other and the whole idea, and had stopped laughing. We had planned our opening line, and felt that after going through the preparation and practice we were looking forward to the main event and some fun.

As we rounded the corner and could see the chairs in the lobby, we knew who our victim was. He was sitting in a chair facing the direction we were coming, with a look on his face of "shock and awe," many, many, many, years before "shock and awe," was even a concept. Poor Ray, mouth open, eyes wide, he watched in disbelief and horror, as Marilyn and I came towards him.

Danny, with help from Janet, was trying very hard not to laugh. Obviously word of mouth had spread because there were about 100 girls throughout the lobby...watching. No words, no sound was coming from Ray. I started, "Hi, I'm Jana." "I'm Marilyn," Marilyn said, "We are Siamese Twins," we said together. I concluded it with, "and we only have one heart."

What was Ray to do? He wanted to run away screaming, I am sure. But being the good sport he was he didn't, although I don't know if it was because he was just a good sport, or if he was paralyzed and couldn't move. Finally Janet suggested, because Danny couldn't talk for laughing so hard, that we better get going.

Now Ray had a chance to run, but he stayed, but now he had another problem. He did not know where to walk. Should he walk in front of us, behind us, with us? His choice was in front of us. Marilyn, Janet, and I are talking away, and finally Ray comes back to us, and says, "I think there might be a problem, I have bucket seats." I said very calmly, "That's okay, we are used to it." After saying that I began to try to figure out if I was the bucket twin or not, and as it turned out I was. It was one of the most uncomfortable rides for my bottom in my life. As soon as we are in the car, Marilyn and I started fighting over the fact that she had the heart and I claimed that she had always wanted to kill me to have her heart to herself. Ray is driving in total silence and looking sicker and sicker as we drive.

This whole time Danny is trying not to laugh, but not doing a very good job of it, as he and Janet are sitting in the back seat. Finally, I think to get us to stop fighting over the one heart, Ray speaks, "So what is your major?" We had not prepared for that one. We answered separately, "I am in Speech and Theater," I said. Marilyn, said, "And I am in Home Economics." Ray had a very puzzled look on his face, and he said, "Well isn't that hard, I mean two majors?" I answered before Marilyn had a chance, "Yes, it is, we have to go to twice as many classes, and when I am doing a scene in theater class or doing a play, we have to put a sheet over Marilyn." That response shut Ray right up and the rest of the drive to the rodeo was in complete silence.

Marilyn and I had decided that we didn't want to go to the rodeo as Siamese twins so she had brought a seam ripper to disconnect us. Ray did not realize this and asked us what would happen when we got to the Phoenix Coliseum, because he realized that there would be individual seating. We stated that it was no problem that they knew us and made arrangements for us.

As soon as we got to the Coliseum Ray got out of his car and went around like the good gentleman he was and opened the door for us. Marilyn got out first and then I got out and in unison, we said, "Surprise, surprise, surprise." Ray took one look at Danny, and said, "Danny, I am going to kill you." He didn't and he took us to the rodeo and out to eat after the rodeo and suggested that he had a friend that he would love for us to go out with as Siamese twins. Marilyn and I both declined as our Siamese twins days were over. We asked Ray if he believed our stunt, or if he believed that we were truly Siamese twins, and he said he did wonder, but was afraid to say anything in case it was true.

Today, in 2006, I don't know what has happened to Marilyn, Janet, or Ray, Danny died 15 to 20 years ago, but I do believe that they all remember the Siamese twin date as much as I do and all the fun and laughter we got from it. It is one of those times when I am so glad that we allowed our child out and played and laughed.

As I mentioned before I majored in Speech and Theater and for some reason I always played funny old women, I figure now that I am getting to that age I will really know how to play the part. In fact, I am proud to announce that I am founder and president of a new group, and some of you can join my group, and some of you will have to wait. The name of my group is Slightly Older Sex Objects, or SO SO's for short. Our motto is "You are only young once, but you can be SO SO forever."

My life is a joke. This is another way that viewing my life as a joke helps me to handle getting older and to be able to laugh at it, because the alternative for getting older doesn't seem too funny at this point.

PLAY 272

Take My Husband Please...

Not everything faced can be changed, but nothing can
be changed until it is faced.
James Baldwin

While in college I met my ex-husband,
and I should have realized immediately
that it would not work. We had so many
differences, he was always right, and
walked on water; I was always wrong, and
retained water. He stood up to pee and I
sat down. He's Jewish, and I was
Mormon. We compromised, we raised the
kids Jewish, and I got to pick out the
names, Brigham Young and Joseph Smith.
Now Brigham Young didn't like that name
for a long time, but now she does. I think
these are the only two children I have, or
at least that I know of.

The hardest part of having kids for me,
was getting used to all the yelling,
screaming and crying that went on for the

first couple of years until I learned to control myself.

The biggest difference between my ex-husband and me, and probably why we got divorced, is that I viewed my life as a joke, and he viewed his life as way too serious. I laughed at things that happened to me, and he stressed about everything. At the end of our marriage I was losing, I was starting to see my life as a bad joke, instead of the good joke that it was.

So after 13 years of marriage, my husband Richard, who I affectionately called Dick, put magic into my life by disappearing. There was one thing that Dick and I shared in our marriage, we both loved him.

After the divorce I realized that viewing my life as a joke and laughing at it was necessary for me and for Brigham Young and Joseph Smith, to survive and be in the present moment and plan the future instead of living in the past.

And during this time I gained weight. And, I want you to know that I have tried many diets. I tried the banana coconut diet. I haven't lost any weight but I can sure climb those trees. I went on an onion, garlic, and Limburger cheese diet, again, no weight lose, but you know what, from a distance I look thinner. People say, "Jana," because that's my name "Jana, have you lost weight," and I say, "Yes, Yes, but don't get any closer." My Mom, before she passed away, said "Jana," because that's my name, "the best way to lose weight is to eat naked in front of a mirror." I tried it, I did. It works but unfortunately, I can't get back to Denny's.

Part 2

A Playbook for Life

PLAY 121550

P.L.A.Y.S.

Intellect is the ability to play with ideas
Albert Einstein

To help the participants in my workshops, and the audiences in my presentations, I created a method or technique of bringing more laughter, fun, creativity, and joy into their lives. This technique is an acronym called P.L.A.Y.S.. P.L.A.Y.S is easy to remember and each letter stands for a word or concept that is also easy to remember. The acronym P.L.A.Y.S. is P stands for Play, L stands for Laughter, A is for Attitude, Y is for Yippee, and S stands for Smile.

In Part 2 of this book I will be taking each letter in P.L.A.Y.S. and address ways to bring more of it into your life. The more you can share Oscar Wilde's view of "Life is too important to take seriously," the happier you will be.

One of the very nice benefits of P.L.A.Y.S. is the interconnection with all the words or concepts. For instance, if you are playing, more than likely you will be laughing, have a good attitude, wanting to shout YIPPEE, and be smiling too. And if you are smiling, you will more than likely be in a good mood, close to laughing, might be playing, and thinking YIPPEE to life. This interconnection works across the board.

PLAY 1113

P-PLAY

You can discover more about a person in an hour of play than in a year of conversation.
Plato

For many adults PLAY is considered the domain of children. Children play, adults work. We even tell people to "quit playing around," "quit playing games with me," "he/she is playing with my mind." Play for an adult is too often considered a dirty word. I think that in fact play is the domain of being human; although that's not totally true because most animals play, have you ever watched dogs, or cats at play. So maybe play is the domain of being alive. Albert Einstein said, "Intellect is the ability to play with ideas." Play is every important on many levels.

I am always asking my audiences who look or seem happier, adults or children. The answer always comes back, children seem happier. Then almost immediately, people want to qualify why children seem happier they say "yes, but kids don't have to work, they don't have responsibilities, they have no worries." Which I always reply with, "yes, and they also have no power, people are always telling them what to do and when." So instead of telling children and adults to "grow-up," I think we should tell people to "grow-down," children seem much happier.

My theory is that children seem or are happier because they are always playing, and we know from research that only 12 adults out of a 100 take any time to play during the week. What this means is that 82 adults out of 100 don't play at all during the week. And how many times are those 12 playing? That is not reported. I hope that it is more than once.

I have two children, whom I know of, and when they were small, and I would give them a toy, many times they played with the box. My children were always playing; from the time they got up in the morning until they finally fell asleep at night.

As Albert Einstein said at the beginning of this Play that, "intellect is the ability to play with ideas." Part of my children's play was the extensive use of their imaginations. They were discovering the world and their place in it by playing with ideas, and the way they did that was through their imagination.

As adults, we quit playing, then we quit using our imaginations, and we stop being creative and innovative. A study was done with 4 year olds that found 98 percent of them were creative, when those 4 year olds reached 16; about 17 percent of them were creative. What happened? My belief is that by 16, many teenagers have already stopped playing and using their imaginations as much.

The Ways and Whys of Play

So what are some ways or methods of bringing play back into your life? I think the first way is to be aware of the importance of play. One of the best ways is to be come aware of your beliefs about work. Below is a comparison list to compare work with its opposite word play. Write one word under Work, that represents *work* to you and write one word under <u>Play</u> that represents *play* to you. I have started it for you.

Comparison List

Work	Play
Hard	Fun

Most people find that the more positive, joyful words are under Play, instead of Work. So the key is to bring more *play* into *work*. So how is that done? One way is to change your attitude about work. Dr. Annette Goodheart, says to bring the "perks" of fun and laughter into work, and instead of calling work, "Work," call it "Plerk." Dr. Goodheart points out that calling "Work," "Plerk," makes it sound so much better. I think, you can than tell people not to brother you as you will be "Plerking" all day.

People spend 2/3 of their lives working, so you need to make sure you are "Plerking," at a job that you like. Too many people live for the weekend or retirement. I had a co-worker who was constantly complaining about her job, she walked around each day telling everyone how much she hated her job, she said, "I hate my job, I hate my job, do you like your job? I hate mine." One day, in a very calm voice, I said, "SHUT UP! Find another job; there are many jobs out there. Find something you like." In a very calm manner, she said, "No, Jana," because that's my name, "no, Jana, that is okay, I only have 15 years until I retire." I got another job. I was tired of listening to her complain. If you don't like your job, please find another one. Life is too short to be miserable in a job you don't like.

So besides changing your attitude how else can you bring more play into your life? Another way to bring play into your life is by taking a blank sheet of paper and at the top writing Twenty Things I Love to Do and then listing 20 separate things that you love doing. This can include things, like walking, eating, sleeping, sex (yes, include it) any activity that gives you pleasure or joy. After listing the 20 items indicate how frequently you participate in the activity and whether it is an activity you do alone or with others. For some or all the activities you can answer both alone and with others (including sex), if you do both. I have provided an example below for you to complete.

Twenty Things I Love to Do

Activity	Daily- Weekly- Monthly- Yearly	Alone- With Others
1.		
2.		
3.		
4.		
5.		
6.		
7.		
8.		
9.		
10		
11.		
12		
13		
14		
15.		
16.		
17		
18.		
19.		
20.		

Some people have trouble creating this list, and can only list eight to ten items, which may indicate that they don't have much joy in their lives. As Woody Allen said, "You might as well enjoy life, as you won't get out of it alive anyway."

By creating a list of Twenty Things That You Love to Do, and making sure every day that you are doing a minimum of two of these things, you are bringing *play* back into your life. When we enjoy what we are doing, it is always play and never work. Two things that I love doing are laughing and reading. So each day I make sure I laugh for at least five minutes, (in the next PLAY we will talk about how to laugh when you have nothing to laugh at), and read for at least a half hour.

"Sharpen the Saw" is Habit 7 in Stephen Covey's, *The 7 Habits of Highly Effective People*. "To Sharpen the Saw," means that you have to be constantly renewing and taking care of yourself. One of the best ways to renew and take care of yourself is to do those things that you love, or to *Play*.

Besides <u>Attitude</u>, and <u>The Twenty Things</u> <u>I Love to Do List</u>, another way of bringing more play into your life is to, at least once a year, if not more, schedule a whole day where you have nothing planned, and spend that day as a child would. Get rid of your watch, cell phone, any distractions, and just play all day, without a schedule. Just do whatever pops into your head. If you want to sleep all day, allow yourself to do that. If you want to run naked around the house, go for it, perhaps getting permission, or giving warnings to whoever needs them. Live totally in the moment for that entire day. This is your chance, once a year to live like a child again and play all day. This one act will create major dividends, for your well-being and you will rediscover the power of play.

Finally, I think that it is very interesting that we call both actors and athletes *Players*. We have baseball, basketball, and football *players*. A group of actors are many times called *Players*, who do *Plays*. We don't say the baseball *worker*, or she/he is in a Broadway *Work*. So what I am suggesting is that as much as possible bring more *play* into your life.

Play With These Ideas

❖ Change your attitude towards work, and life and if you can't change your attitude, change your job or life.

❖ Put more "Plerk" (perks of fun and laughter at work) into your work.

❖ Complete your <u>Twenty Things I Love to Do</u> list and do a minimum of two things each day.

❖ Spend at least one day a year without a watch, cell phone, or schedule and just play all day.

❖ Be in the present moment as much as possible. We only have this moment and no other.

❖ Play with your children or grandchildren, they can teach you how to play.

❖ Look for play and it will find you.

❖ Practice playing. The more you play the better you get at it and the more you do it.

Your Page to Play With

PLAY 0216

L-LAUGHTER

We are all here for a spell. Get all the good laughs you can.
Mark Twain

- ✓ Increases antibodies in saliva that combats upper respiratory infections.
- ✓ Decreases serum cortical, thus providing an antidote for the harmful effects of stress.
- ✓ Secretes an enzyme that protects the stomach from forming ulcers.
- ✓ Conditions the abdominal muscles.
- ✓ Relaxes muscles throughout the body.
- ✓ Aids in reducing symptoms of neuralgia and rheumatism.
- ✓ Changes perspective.
- ✓ Has a positive benefit on mental functions.
- ✓ Improves ventilation, thus helping reduce chronic respiratory conditions.
- ✓ Reduces blood pressure and heart rate.

✓ Liberates interleukin-2 and other immune boosters.
✓ Helps the body fight infection.
✓ Releases endorphins, which provide natural pain relief.
✓ Helps move nutrients and oxygen to body tissues.

Wow! What provides you with all these benefits? The answer is *laughter*. Laughter has been referred to as "Internal Jogging." If you are like me and whenever you feel like exercising you just lay down to the thought goes away than laugher is for you. There are some researchers who estimate that laughing 100 times is as much of a workout as 15 minutes on an exercise bike. To laugh 100 times a day seems extreme especially when you consider that most adults only laugh 8 to 15 times a day. Of course, we all know how to laugh more, considering that children laugh between 300 to 400 times in a day.

So what happened, why did you go from 300 to 400 times a day laughing, as children, to only 8 to 15 times a day as a an adult? Most people give the following reasons: work, responsibilities, growing up, there being nothing to laugh at. Children, many people tell me have no responsibilities, so it is easy for them to laugh. That is true, but it is also true that they have no power. Whether we *laugh* or not is solely dependent on our deciding to *laugh* or not, just as whether we *play* or not is dependent on the choices we make.

Benefits of Laughter

As the creator of your life, you determine how you live your life. And those decisions include whether you *play* or *laugh.* One of the major myths that stop all of us from laughing is that we have to have a reason. Humor is intellect, while laughter is physical and requires no reason. Babies laugh and their intellect is not developed enough for them to have a reason for their laughter. William James said it best when he said, "We don't laugh because we are happy, we are happy because we laugh." For some of us if we waited until we were happy we would never laugh.

Norman Cousins, in his book, *Anatomy of an Illness*, related his experience of using laughter to conquer his painful and potentially terminal illness. He found that if he could laugh for ten minutes, he could sleep for two hours of pain-free sleep; without the laughter he was unable to sleep. Believing that negative emotions had caused him to get sick, he thought that positive emotions might make him well and it did. He lived for another 25 to 30 years.

His book documents his treatment program of laughter, and when blood tests showed that his sedimentation rate dropped several points, after each laugh episode, he totally believed the old saying that "laughter is the best medicine." He would bring in movies of the *Marx Brothers*, and *The Three Stooges*, and laugh and laugh. Ironically, they kicked Norman out of the hospital for making too much noise and he had to finish his treatment in a hotel room.

Norman Cousins and his book, *Anatomy of an Illness*, started a Laughter Revolution and led to much research that has found all the benefits of laughter mentioned at

the start of this *PLAY*. As mentioned
earlier in the *PLAY* research has
established the existence of substances in
the brain called endorphins that have a
molecular structure very much like
morphine. Endorphins are natural "uppers"
and natural relaxants. We know now that
laughter stimulates our brain to produce
an alertness hormone called
catecholamine, which in turn stimulates
the release of endorphins into our
bloodstream.

One person who has been studying the
benefits of laughter for many years is Dr.
Lee Berk, a professor of Pathology and
Laboratory medicine at Loma Linda
University in California. Dr. Berk believes,
"if we took what we now know about
laughter and bottled it, it would require
FDA approval." Studies by Dr. Berk and
Dr. Stanley Tan, also of Loma Linda have
shown that laughing lowers blood pressure,
increases muscle flexion and triggers a
flood of beta-endorphins, the brain's
natural morphine like compounds that can
induce a sense of euphoria.

The most profound effects of laughter
occur on the immune system. During

laughter natural killer cells that destroy viruses and tumors increase. Gamma-interferon, a disease-fighting protein, rises with laughter, as do B-cells, which produce disease-destroying antibodies, and T-cells, which orchestrate the immune response.

Dr. Tan has found that laughter provides a safety valve that shuts off the flow of stress hormones, the flight or fight compounds that come into play during times of stress, hostility, and rage.

As mentioned earlier it has also been found from some researchers that laughing 100 times is as much of a workout as 15 minutes on an exercise bike. That laughter is a full body workout. Laughter exercises the cardiovascular system by lowering blood pressure and increasing heart rate, which any aerobic exercise will do. It also probably improves the coordination of brain functions, which increases alertness and memory and helps clear the respiratory tract from coughing. Laughter increases blood oxygen: and strengthens internal muscles by tightening and releasing them. One doctor has said that

20 seconds of laughing works the heart as hard as three minutes of hard rowing. This might not be totally true but we do know that laughing does give your body a workout.

Dr. Beck sums up his research on the benefits of laughter this way: "Blessed are those who laugh, for they shall last."

So where is laughter beneficial or appropriate? My answer is everywhere. Yes, even at work and funerals, and hopefully the environment at your work is not like a funeral. If so, it is best to change your job. In fact any extreme emotion can make people laugh, that is why people do laugh at funerals. I found it interesting that funeral has FUN in it. Not really sure what that means, just an observation.

What's So Funny?

Laughter is an emotional response, without reason, and extremely subjective. Psychologist Patricia Keith-Spiegel has identified the following eight major theories on "Why We Laugh."

1. **Surprise-** We laugh most often to cover our feelings of embarrassment. This is a result of either having unintentionally done or said something foolish or having been tricked. Laughing because we are surprised is the most universally reason we laugh.

2. **Superiority-** There appears to be a strong and constant need for us to feel superior, hence all the jokes that make fun of people (blond jokes, polish jokes). Humor is a reaction to tragedy. "The joke is at someone else's expense," wrote Alan Dundes.

3. **Biological-** This theory states that laughter is something we are born with. It is a function of the nervous system to stimulate, relax, and restore a feeling of well-being

4. **Incongruity-** According to Henri Bergson, a person laughs at incongruity when there is unconventional pairing of actions or thoughts.

    Conrad Hilton, the hotel magnate, was asked to broadcast his New Year's wish. "I wish everyone would make a New Year's resolution to please put the shower curtain inside the tub."

5. **Ambivalence-** The theory is similar to incongruity in its dependence on incompatible experiences. However, where incongruity tends to stress clashing ideas of perception, ambivalence stresses conflicting

emotions, such as love/hate relationships in families.

Whatever happened to the good ol days, when children worked in factories?
Emo Philips

6.   **Release-** We laugh to release or reduce the stress that we feel. Our hope is that laughter will help us get rid of our anxieties; especially if fortified by group approval.

Instead of working for the survival of the fittest, we should be working for the survival of the wittiest, and then we can all die laughing.
Lily Tomlin

7.   **Configuration-** We smile, frequently even laugh out loud, when we experience that sudden insight of having solved a mystery or figured out something. We laugh when the material encourages us to

complete some missing
information.

I learned about sex the hard
way- from books.
Emo Philips

8. Psychoanalytical- Freud's
theory of laughter contended
that the ludicrous always
represents a "saving in the
expenditure of psychic energy."
"We laugh in order to socially
accomplish childish regression
without being foolish," wrote
Flugel. We can learn a great
deal about our own psychological
makeup by constantly asking
ourselves, "Why did I laugh at
this joke and not at that one?"

We're young only once, but
with humor, we can be
immature forever.
Art Gliner

How to Laugh

One of the major myths of laughter is that we have to have a reason to laugh. Again, laughter is physical and requires no reason. In fact, laughter is unreasonable, illogical, and irrational. It can't be explained and trying to dissect laughter is like dissecting a frog and then expecting it to live. By dissecting laughter too much we kill it. The other two myths of laughter are that we have to be happy to laugh, and that we have to have a sense of humor to laugh. These are wrong on all accounts, and hence classified as myths.

Charlie Chaplin said that, "Laughter is caused by playing with pain." Again notice the connection between play and laughter. Many researchers and scientists point out that laughter can come out of tension, stress, and pain. Laughter can be very therapeutic, as already discussed

So if you wanted to laugh how you would go about doing that? The answer is just laugh. The great news is that the body is fairly stupid and doesn't know the different between real and fake. So even if you just say, "Tee Hee, Tee Hee, Ho, Ho, Ho, Ho, Ha, Ha, Ha, Ha, and pretend to laugh the body thinks you are laughing and releases endorphins, which as mentioned make you feel better. Again, as adults, we have so forgotten to laugh, and too often we walk around with frowns on our faces. The body and mind believe the frown on the face and assume that you must be miserable. The body believes whatever we think, show, or tell it. So if we go through the day laughing and smiling more than frowning and crying, we will automatically feel happier.

Dr. Annette Goodheart in her book, *Laughter Therapy: How to Laugh about Everything in Your Life That Isn't Really Funny*, gives a wonderful example of how to laugh. She says to state whatever is bothering you and then say TEE HEE, TEE HEE, and than laugh. Again, the mind and body don't know the difference between real and fake, and the laugh reminders us that we can't always control our stress but we can always reduce it through laughter.

For about 20 years around the Christmas season I would come down with either a very bad case of the flu or strep throat. I believe that it was caused by the stress of the season, then in 1989 I had the good fortune of seeing Dr. Annette Goodheart in a workshop and she pointed out that people get the same symptoms when they cry as when they have a cold. Their eyes water, their throat gets clogged up, their nose runs. Her belief is the same as other physicians, like Dr. Bernie Siegel, who believe that when we hold in our emotions and don't deal with them, they can, make us sick. Dr. Goodheart points out that if we would laugh and cry more we would not get as many colds and upper respiratory problems.

Well I decided to try out her suggestion and method, and whenever I felt stress I would say whatever was bothering me, and then TEE HEE, TEE HEE, and laugh.

The thing that was bothering me at that time was that I hated my job, so I would drive on the freeway into work in the morning and at night, and say, "I hate my job, TEE HEE, TEE HEE," and laugh. I really got into it. Pretty soon I was waving at passing cars and really laughing. To this day I can start laughing for no reason and really get laughing.

Well, the most amazing thing happened that Christmas I did not get sick and I am happy to say that 17 years later I have not had a bad cause of the flu or strep throat. I did get another job about a year later and while I was at the job I hated, laughing reduced my stress and made me feel better. To this day, if I feel a cold coming on or I have been under quite a bit of stress I just start laughing. Now I don't even need the TEE HEE.

<u>Laugh and Stick Together</u>

I had just completed facilitating a three week Job Readiness Training program, and at the graduation the husband of one of my students came up to me and said, "I want to thank you, Jana," because that's my name, "I want to thank you Jana for saving my marriage." How I thought had I accomplished that? I asked him, "How did I do that?" He said that before his wife took my class they were seriously contemplating divorce, and as soon as she came into my class, she started going home every night sharing with him all the crazy things I had said and done in class.

Remember I have a "Joke Disorder," and I totally believe that all learning experiences must be fun and full of laughter for people to learn. Anyway, he said that he and his wife started laughing together, something they had not done for months, perhaps years, and the laughing lead to them talking, something they had stopped doing along with the laughing. He said, "My wife and I are really talking, and discovering all the reasons anew that brought us together in the first place. Thanks, Jana, I really do believe that you and the laughter you brought to my wife, and her to me, saved our marriage." And to think all I was trying to do was to help her find a job. To be honest, I can't remember if she found a job, but at least she had her marriage saved.

This was interesting to me, at the time, and again I realized the power of laughter. Since that time more research has been done, and Victor Borge's quote of "Laughter being the shortest distance between two people," is proving to be true. The following is from an article entitled: *"The Benefits of Laughing: Why laughter may be the best way to warm up a relationship"* by Hara Estroff Marano in *"Psychology Today:"*

> "But homegrown laughter may be what ailing couples need most. Uniquely human, laughter is, first and foremost, a social signal--it disappears when there is no audience, which may be as small as one other person--and it binds people together. It synchronizes the brains of speaker and listener so that they are emotionally attuned.

Another researcher Robert Provine, Ph.D., a neuroscientist came to similar conclusions, and he found "that laughter is far too fragile to dissect in the laboratory." Instead, he observed thousands of incidents of laughter spontaneously occurring in everyday life, and wittily reports the results in

Laughter: A Scientific Investigation
(Penguin Books, 2001).

"Laughter establishes--or restores--a positive emotional climate and a sense of connection between two people, who literally take pleasure in the company of each other."

For if there's one thing Dr. Provine found it's that speakers laugh even more than their listeners. Of course levity can defuse anger and anxiety, and in so doing it can pave the path to intimacy.

Most of what makes people laugh is not thigh-slapper stuff but conversational comments. "Laughter is not primarily about humor," says Dr. Provine, "but about social relationships."

Among some of his surprising findings:

- The much vaunted health benefits of laughter are probably coincidental, a consequence of it's much more important primary goal: bringing people together. In fact, the health benefits of laughter may result from the social support it stimulates.

- Laughter plays a big role in mating. Men like women who laugh heartily in their presence.

- Both sexes laugh a lot, but females laugh more--126 percent more than their male counterparts. Men are more laugh-getters.

- The laughter of the female is the critical index of a healthy relationship.

- Laughter in relationships declines dramatically as people age.

- Like yawning, laughter is contagious; the laughter of others is irresistible.

So the next time you have an argument with your mate, don't walk out of the room and slam the door. Find a way to laugh with him or her.

It won't make problems go away. But it can set the stage for tackling them together.

Laughing at Work

Too many of us think we have to wait for the weekend or even retirement before we can play, and laugh. Laughter and play are very strongly connected and there is still a thought that if people are laughing at work then they must not be working, they most be playing. Numerous studies have proven the opposite. "Joking on the job has also been known to stimulate creative thinking, prevent burnout, generate loyalty, and increase productivity. The more fun you have, the more you can get done," says Bruce Baum, professor of Exceptional Education at Buffalo State University. Other research is finding that not only can laughter reduce stress and help produce happier, healthier employees, but it can also enhance people's ability to retain and recall information and connect and cooperate with one another. So as mentioned in PLAY 1113, play, play, and play, and that way you will laugh, laugh, and laugh.

So besides playing more at work, what are some other ways to bring more laughter into work? I think one of the ways companies are attempting to do that is the increase in "casual dress" days at work. Some other ideas that I have suggested to my workshop participants are:

- Have a "Thanks in Advance" party for an employee on the day he/she joins the organization.

- Celebrate employee birthdays.

- Put together a "stress support kit" that can be handed out (or requested) by an employee under pressure. Contents could include a comedy CD or DVD, a book, candy, chewing gum, a small dartboard, worry beads, etc.

- Put up a "humor board" in the office where people can pin up cartoons, jokes, etc.

- Have a weekly or monthly humor contest where people for $1 or $2, submit a joke or cartoon, and everyone in the contest votes on them and the winner gets the money.

- From the humor contest keep a "Humor Book" where all the jokes and cartoons can be kept.

- Have an actual "Stress Relief Station," which can be a room or corner at work where the employee can listen to comedy CD's or read funny books, paint, draw, play with clay, or just come to laugh.

- Have everyone in the office write his or her name and a list of what they like (flowers, sports, chocolate, hobbies, etc.) on a slip of paper. Put all the slips in a hat. Each person picks one and becomes that person's "secret pal." This works very good over the holiday season, or do it over a month or two period of time, and make it your mission to do spontaneous, fun, and enlivening things for your partner-anonymously. At the end have a "Public Confession" where everyone finds out who their secret pals are.

- Encourage each other to establish or take a "Call in Well Day" where people can take time to seriously enjoy themselves.

- Have a "Personal Expression Day" where people are encouraged to wear clothes, hats, buttons, and nametags, whatever that shows their mood.

Besides saying TEE HEE, TEE HEE, and just laughing and playing and all the ways mentioned above to bring more laughter into work, how else might you bring laughter into your life?

Listed below are other ways to bring more laughter into your life:

➢ Read or collect humorous material from your favorite comedy writers and comedians.

➢ Collect cartoons and jokes you enjoy from the internet, newspapers, magazines, etc. Share these with your friends, co-workers, and family, and even complete strangers.

➢ Pledge to yourself that every person you run across during the day you will help smile or laugh.

➢ Use exaggeration to help get perspective. Jokingly expand the situation to life and death proportions.

➢ Be more playful. Try being dramatic, silly, and improvisational. Others will pick up your spirit and laughter.

➢ Remember personal stories from your own lives that, in retrospect, are humorous. Offer these anecdotes as an antidote when others encounter problems.

➢ When an embarrassing moment happens to you share it with your friends and family.

➢ Create a humorous motto to remind yourself and receive parole from the serious situations you may encounter. i.e.: "Soon as you get to the top of the ladder, you discover it's leaning against the wrong wall."

➢ Observe and play with pets to divert attention and release tension.

➢ Create regular times to share humor with friends and family. Joke around meals, place cartoons in lunch bags, watch comedy shows and movies together.

➢ Wear clown noses to indicate you are upset at other family members.

➢ Write your own and your supervisor's job description with obvious exaggeration and perhaps subtle sarcasm.

➢ When you hear a joke you like write it down and then tell it to five people during the course of the day.

➢ Make a list of potential stressful situations and prepare humorous responses.

➢ Carry a funny picture, cartoon, or joke, in your wallet or purse and

look at it when you are feeling
depressed.

➤ Hang out with people who laugh and
find joy in their life.

➤ Look for laughter and humor and it
will find you.

Finally do not start or end the day
reading the newspaper or watching or
listening to the news on TV, the Internet,
or radio. What a dreadful way of
beginning and ending the day. Besides the
NEWS is not really anything NEW, I
think we should call it the OLDS.

So laughing may be one of the most
important things you do. It is good
exercise, and it will make you feel better.
So I challenge you to laugh closer to
children's 300 to 400 times a day instead
of adult's 8 to 15. Please, please GROW
DOWN, and live healthier and happier.

And Finally....

Dr. Ruth's (No I am not a doctor but it sounds good) 10 Ways to Relieve Work Stress

1. Don't Work.
2. Take a Deep Breath and Hold it Till You Pass out.
3. Set the Boss's Wastebasket on Fire
4. Smile and if anyone asks you why you are smiling say, "I smile because I don't know what the hell is going on here."
5. Call in Sick when in fact you are well.
6. Bribe a co-worker to do all your work.
7. Eat garlic and onions so no one will get close enough to tell if you are working.
8. Take vacation time every Day
9. Marry a rich spouse
10. Put "Plerk" (the perks of humor and play in work) into your Work.

Play with These Ideas

- ❖ Give yourself permission to laugh and without a reason.

- ❖ Believe in the power of laughter. Belief is an important ingredient in any health regime. Laughter is a positive emotion, along with hope, love, faith, determination, purpose, and a strong will to live.

- ❖ Substitute connecting humor, cosmic humor, and creative humor for hostile, aggressive, and disconnecting humor.

- ❖ Spend more time with people who already laugh a great deal.

- ❖ Laugh out loud when you watch your favorite comedies or when something funny happens.

- ❖ Start a notebook full of anecdotes, jokes, and cartoons that make you laugh.

❖ Say TEE-HEE aloud and laugh when something gets too serious.

❖ When something funny or embarrassing happens to you during the day, share it with your family and friends and laugh together about it.

❖ Play more? If you don't remember how, watch a three year old.

❖ Most important of all: Practice, Practice, and Practice. Laughter is one of our few natural resources that we lose if we don't use.

Your Page to Play With

Play 0419

A-Attitude

Watch your thoughts; they become words. Watch your words; they become actions. Watch your actions; they become habits. Watch your habits; they become character. Watch your character; it becomes your destiny.
Frank Outlaw

Even before the hit sleeper movie, "What the Bleep Do We Know!?", a couple of years ago, and Quantum Physics, many writers and scholars and scientists wrote about how important a positive attitude is. There were many books written about a hundred years ago with the same message. Some of the titles of these books were: *The Power of Positive Thinking*, *Think and Grow Rich*, and *As a Man Thinketh*. More recent all the major motivational and self-help writers and speakers, Tony Robbins, Stephen Covey, Louise Hay, Dr. Deepak Chopra and Dr. Wayne Dyer to name a few, write about the importance of a positive attitude.

Positive Attitude for Health

As recent as October 16, 2006, research has found that optimism is good for the heart. The most optimistic among a group of 545 Dutch men, age 64 to 84, had a roughly 50 percent lower risk of cardiovascular death over 15 years of follow-up, according to a study published in the Archives of Internal Medicine.

Previous research has suggested that being optimistic boosts overall physical health and lowers the risk of death from all causes. A positive attitude also has been shown to help patients who suffer from heart disease caused by narrowed arteries.

This new study measured participants' level of optimism about their lives by having them respond to statements such as "I do not look forward to what lies ahead for me in the years to come" or "My days seem to be passing by slowly" or "I am still full of plans."

"Optimism can be estimated easily and is stable over long periods, though it does tend to decrease with age," said lead researcher Erik Giltay of the Institute of Mental Health in Deft, in the Netherlands.

On a scale of zero to three, with three being most optimistic, the average scores in the study fell from 1.5 in 1985 to 1.3 in 2000.

Higher scores were associated with being younger, being better educated, and living with others, having better health, and doing more physical activity.

"It is yet to be established whether interventions aimed at improving an older individual's level of optimism may reduce the risk of cardiovascular mortality," he added.

More recent work by psychologist Martin E. P. Seligman, as detailed in his book *Learned Optimism: How to Change Your Mind and Your Life*, plus the recent work on the study of Happiness is finding that our genes do play a part in whether we are naturally positive or negative. However, Dr. Seligman, plus other researches and scientists are finding that we do have control over our thoughts and feelings, and the first step is awareness.

All of this new research ties in with both Emotional Intelligence and now, Social Intelligence, which suggest that successful people have an awareness of their own thoughts and feelings and have empathy for others. If I can know myself and be aware of what I am thinking and feeling I can work on being more positive. We know that our thoughts create our feelings and visa versa. As William James put it, "The greatest discovery of my generation is that a human being can alter his life by altering his attitudes."

Affirmations

So how do you do that? One of the best ways I know is through Affirmations. Affirmations came from the field of counseling as a way to replace negative thoughts into positive thoughts. For every 1 negative thing you say to someone, or yourself, to erase it from your mind you have to say 12 positive things. So the more affirmations you can say to yourself the better.

There are some guidelines for affirmations; first they need to be in the present tense, personal, realistic, and not written to compare yourself with someone else. Example: I, Jana, am a wonderful person.

I have enclosed some affirmations below:

- I _____ am on the right track.
- I _____ am doing extremely well.
- I _____ am having a great time.
- I _____ love and approve of myself.
- I _____ attract money into my life.
- I _____ know that life is really good for me.
- I _____ am moving into what I am wanting.
- I _____ am where I am supposed to be right now.
- I _____ trust in the process of life.
- I _____ am a money magnet.
- I _____ am willing to change for the better.
- I _____ deserve the best and I accept it now.
- I _____ am healthy and happy.
- I _____ love my body and myself just the way I am.

Notice that the affirmation is in the present tense, not someday I will love myself, or be a money magnet when all the planets are in alignment. Your brain is amazing and it listens to you, and it instructs the body. If you tell your mind and body "I am wonderful," both your mind and body will believe you. If you tell your mind and body that someday "I will be wonderful," your body and mind don't know what someday is and won't listen. To your mind and body the only thing they know is the present.

So how often and when are affirmations done? My suggestion is to pick one or two affirmations at a time and to do them for a minimum of 21 days, which is how long it takes to change any habit. Good times are the morning and before bed, best time is all day. Louise Hay, in her book, *Heal Your Life* suggests all day long. She says the more that you say affirmations the faster they work. Do your affirmations with feeling. Remember that thoughts with strong feelings cause actions and behaviors.

Presentism

In his book, *Stumbling on Happiness Think You Know What Makes You Happy?* Daniel Gilbert says that recent brain research has found what he is calling "presentism" which is the tendency for current experience to influence one's views of the past and the future. Daniel Gilbert contends, in his book that the human being is the only animal that thinks about the future. So we may think about the future, but what we are doing is projecting into the future what we are thinking and feeling today. As Daniel Gilbert said is his book, "More simply said, most of us have a tough time imagining a tomorrow that is terribly different from today, and we find it particularly difficult to imagine that we will ever think, want, or feel differently than we do now."

Now is All We Have

A couple of years ago when my Mom got very ill, and about eight months before she passed away, to get through it I had to be in the NOW. I was very thankful for being in theater in college and learning to be in the present moment. In theater you learn that you must be in the present moment because you never know what might happen. For example someone might forget a line, a prop might not be where it is suppose to be or the scenery may fall down, and if you are thinking about your last line or your upcoming line you are sure to mess up. Because after all, NOW is all you have, whether in the theater or life. As the saying goes, "yesterday is history, and tomorrow is a mystery so all we have is the present, which is why we call it a gift."

So many of us live in the past thinking either about how terrible or wonderful it was, and we bring it with us into the present, and then to make matters worse, we project that past into the future. Added to that is then the negative thoughts and affirmations we say, "I haven't ever had a job that paid me enough, or used my talent and I know I never will. Well you would be right. As Henry Ford said, "If you think you can, you can, and if you think you can't you're right." By having positive thoughts today, you are assuring yourself of positive thoughts tomorrow. Deepak Chopra says that 90 percent of the thoughts we have tomorrow will be the thoughts we had today.

Thoughts like feelings and actions become habits. In fact thoughts and feelings lead to certain behaviors and actions. If you really want to know what you really believe, simply watch what you do. So if you want to change your actions and behaviors you need to change your thoughts and feelings. The only time you have is the present time, and it is the only time you have control over. To live in the present you need to be aware of it and focus your attention on it.

Focusing Attention

The Law of Attraction says that what you focus on is what you get. If you want health, wealth, and happiness you need to focus on that. If you focus on what you don't have you get more of that. *What you think upon grows*. This is an Eastern maxim and it summons up The Law of Attraction. *What you think upon grows.* Whatever you allow to occupy your mind you magnify in your own life. Whether the subject of your thought is good or bad, The Law of Attraction works and the condition grows. Any thing that you keep out of your mind tends to diminish or disappear in you life.

The more you think about your grievances or the injustices that you have suffered, the more such trials you will continue to receive; the more you think of the good fortune you have had, the more good fortune will come to you. The Law of Attraction is *what you think upon grows.*

If you want to have a positive attitude, if you want to have happiness, if you want health and wealth then focus on those, be grateful for those things you have, don't focus on what you don't have.

The Gratitude Journal

One of the best ways to be grateful is to keep a *Gratitude Journal*. The *Gratitude Journal* comes from University of California Psychologist Sonja Lyubominirsky "8 Steps toward a More Satisfying Life;" she says to write down three to five things for which you are currently thankful. Dr. Lyubominirsky says to include the minor things with the major things and to do it once a week, perhaps on Sunday night, and to "keep it fresh by varying your entries as much as possible." The other "7 Steps Toward a More Satisfying Life" are:

1. Practice acts of kindness- Being kind to others, whether friends or strangers, triggers a cascade of positive effects- it makes you feel generous and capable, and gets The Law of Attraction going, you will get back what you give.

2. Savor life's joys- This is being in the moment and paying attention to pleasures and wonders.

3. Thank a mentor- Thank people who have mentored you or been helpful and do it in person.

4. Learn to forgive- Let go of anger and resentment. As Buddy Hacket said, "While I am holding a grudge, the person I am holding the grudge about is out dancing."

5. Invest time and energy in friends and family- The biggest factor, researchers are finding out in what makes people happy and being satisfied with life is having strong personal relationships.

6. Take care of your body- Getting plenty of sleep; exercising, playing, smiling and laughing can all enhance your mood in the short term, and practiced regularly they can help make your daily life more satisfying.

7. Develop strategies for coping with stress and hardships- (The acronym P.L.A.Y.S. -Play-Laughter-Attitude-Yippee-Smile is a perfect strategy and the reason for this book.)

The Victory Log

The Victory Log is a similar concept as *The Gratitude Journal*; except it is to help you keep track of your successes, small and big. I don't know about you but there are some days that just getting out of bed is the best thing I can do. On those days on my *Victory Log* I will put, "Getting out of bed." Try to fill in as many victories as you can each day. Doing this is a great way to remind you that you are doing things and achieving things each and every day. It also is a way for you to focus on the positive things you do each and every day, instead of the negative. An example of The *Victory Log* follows on the next page.

The Victory Log

Please record all victories that you have had today, big and small.

Today' Date: _____

1. _____
2. _____
3. _____
4. _____
5. _____
6. _____
7. _____
8. _____
9. _____
10. _____
11. _____
12. _____
13. _____
14. _____
15. _____

Fake it Till You Make It!

I had been working for eight years teaching tennis and running tennis tournaments and then Dick, my ex-husband put magic into my life by disappearing and I had to get a full-time, professional job. After a year, looking, I landed a job teaching low-income people, mainly women, job finding skills. And let me tell you I felt like a fake, it was the first time in my life that I had to wear professional clothes and this mainly involved wearing skirts and blouses. Now, you have to remember that I was used to wearing shorts and warm-up suits, the farthest from a professional suit that you can think of.

So every day when I got dressed, I would look in the mirror and feel that I looked like a female impersonator. Besides feeling like a female impersonator I, also felt like a fake regarding the material I was supposed to teach. One of my co-workers after I told her my anxiety gave me the best advice I think I have ever gotten. She said, "Jana," because that's my name, "Jana, do what we all do *Fake it till you make it."* Well, that is what I started doing 20 years ago and I haven't stopped since. Remember like I mentioned before your body is stupid and will believe whatever your mind and feelings tell it. So if you say to yourself repeatedly, as I did in an affirmation, "I, Jana am confident. I know what I am doing." "I, Jana am confident. I know what I am doing." You will start to believe yourself. So, when in doubt, "Fake it Till You Make It."

Visualization

Recent scientific studies with the brain indicate that the brain does not know the difference between real and imagined. So if you visualize yourself being successful and happy, you will be. They have found that if a person looks at a picture and they do a CAT scan of the brain, certain parts of the brain will light up. Now the amazing thing is that when that same person thinks of the picture in their mind and a CAT scan is done the same parts of the brain light up. The brain does not know the difference between the real picture and an imagined picture.

"Habit 2" of Stephen Covey's *7 Habits of Highly Effective People* is "Begin with the End in Mind," and it states that in every thing we do we first do it in the mental plane and then in the physical plane. People, who create anything, first do it in their minds and then in the physical world. It goes back to what has been mentioned before in PLAY 1409 that our thoughts create our actions and behaviors.

Athletes use this concept all the time. In fact a study was done that proves how powerful visualizations can do. Three groups of basketball free throw shooters were chosen. All three groups were tested before the experiment began. Group A, after the testing, practiced shooting free throws every day for an hour for two weeks. Group B, after the testing, sat in a room visualizing shooting free throws successfully for an hour each day for two weeks. Group C, after the testing, did nothing, no practicing, and no visualizing, for two weeks. As expected in Group C, there was no improvement, Group A, on the other hand improved by *25 percent*. The most exciting discovery was that Group B, increased by *24 percent* only 1 percent less than Group A, whose members physically practiced every day.

Victor Frankel used this technique to survive a Nazi death camp. He spent his time visualizing giving lectures about his discovery that people could do horrible things to other people, but the one thing they couldn't do to people is control another person's mind or thoughts. Once Victor survived the camp, he did give many lectures, and he felt that his visualizing the experience made it very easy to do. He wrote a very good book about his experience called *Man's Search for Meaning*.

Mission or Purpose Statement

One of the other major discoveries of Victor Frankel's while in the Nazi camp was the importance of a central purpose or mission for your life. He felt that if people had a mission or purpose for their life it was easier for them to survive major crises in their lives. I believe that having a mission or purpose statement for your life helps you set direction and maintain a more positive attitude for your life.

One question that I ask the participants in my playshops is to raise their hands if they plan vacations. Almost every hand goes up, and then I ask them if they have planned their life up to this point. And I do this by asking them these questions: I ask them by a show of hands how many planned the job they have now. Most of the hands go down. I ask for a show of hands for those that planned when and if they got married. Again, not very many hands go up. I ask how many planned the number of children they wanted or didn't want. Again very few hands go up. I ask how many people planned the education they have. At this point fewer hands are in the air then were in the air around planning vacations. I think it is sad that many of us spend more time planning vacations and less time planning our lives. And then we wonder why we are not happy with our lives.

Having a *Mission* or *Purpose Statement* helps set direction for your life and I believe it also helps maintain a more positive attitude. If you have a *Mission* or

Purpose Statement for your life, and you are working at a job you hate, you will discover that many times your job is not matching your *Mission* or *Purpose Statement*, which explains why you don't like your job. This many times will give you the incentive to find another job.

So how do you develop a *Mission or Purpose Statement?* There are many ways and it is important to find the one that works for you. The first step is self-awareness; start paying attention to what excites you. What activities give you energy? Look at your hobbies, those things you do for fun. If at all possible, get away by yourself and journal and ask yourself the above questions. One method that I found extremely helpful was to write out my own obituary. I wrote out all those things I wanted to accomplish in my life and what I wanted people to say about me after I died.

Your *Mission or Purpose Statement* can be as long or short as you want. Each person's is different and unique to them. For me having a *Personal Mission Statement* has really helped me in my life. My *Personal Mission Statement* is: I

<u>Jana bring laughter, play, and happiness
to every person I meet</u>. I once left a job
and found another job because I felt the
job I left was not allowing me to fulfill my
mission or purpose in life. *Mission* or
Purpose Statements are powerful. Please
consider writing a *Mission* or *Purpose
Statement* for yourself, you are worth it.

However if you want to stay miserable
here are 15 ways to do it.

<u>15 Ways to Stay Miserable or How to get There if You Are Not!</u>

1. Wait for others to make you happy.

2. Blame everyone else for your unhappiness.

3. Use "if only" whenever you can regarding time, money or friends.

4. Compare what you have with what others have.

5. Always be serious.

6. Take responsibility for everything bad in the world.

7. Try to please everyone all the time, except yourself, and never say "no."

8. Help others but don't let anyone help you.

9. Consider your own wants unimportant.

10. If anyone compliments you, discount it immediately.

11. Never laugh or play.

12. Hide your own thoughts and feelings.

13. Resist change to the death.

14. Strive for absolute perfection.

15. Always live in the past or in the future never in the present.

Play with These Ideas

o Have a Mission or Purpose Statement for you Life. Put it where you can see it.

o Set goals for yourself and write them down.

o Visualize what you want in life.

o Recognize that the quality and quantity of your life is directly related to the quantity and quality of your thoughts.

o Remember <u>The Law of Attraction</u> you get what you focus on and what you focus on, grows.

o Do affirmations every day.

o Know that you are the creator of your life. You can't always control what happens to you but you can always control how you respond to it.

o Keep a Gratitude Journal and Victory Log.

Your Page to Play With

PLAY 303012

Y-YIPPEE

Whenever I have to choose between two evils, I always like to try the one I haven't tried before.
Mae West

YIPPEE! How Fascinating

What a great attitude by Mae West. Obviously she was not afraid of making mistakes. Making mistakes is what YIPPEE in my acronym is partly about. So I tell people that you should celebrate your mistakes, and the way to do that is borrowed from Benjamin Zander, and Rosamund Stone Zander's book, *The Art of Possibility: Transforming Professional and Personal Life*. So when you make a mistake, put your hands above your head wiggle them and say, 'YIPPEE," and as you put your hands down look around you and say, "How fascinating." This little exercise is to remind you not to take yourself too seriously. It is also to remind you that if you are not making mistakes you are not learning. Anytime, let me repeat this, anytime, you are learning something new you can expect to make mistakes, and mistakes are okay. Just celebrate your mistakes with, YIPPEE! How fascinating.

Learn from Children

As children we have no problem making mistakes, in fact, we go out of our way to make mistakes. That is how we learn. If you have ever watched a baby learning to walk, mistakes is what they do all the time, when they are learning. They take one-step and fall, and they get right up and try again. What do adults do while watching babies learning to walk? We act as their cheering section. We cheer them on. We laugh and applaud each and every attempt. Babies know instinctively that the only way they are going to learn to walk or talk is to failure at it.

I don't know any baby that has stopped trying to walk and said to himself/herself "Okay that is it! I give up. You know there is nothing wrong with crawling. In fact, I like crawling; I can cover much more ground this way and much faster. I am not sure what the big deal is with walking?"

So what happens, why do we have the never give up attitude as babies and so afraid to make a mistake attitude as adults? Again like laughing, playing, having a positive attitude, lack of fear of making mistakes seems to leave us, as we become an adult. Most of us, as adults, try to avoid making mistakes. How often, as an adult do you make a mistake and people around you laugh and offer you encouragement, like we do with babies as they are learning to walk or talk. Won't it be great when we are learning a new skill to have people offer support and encouragement? Instead we get disapproval looks, or in some situations, we are actually punished for making mistakes.

Many times we find that the older we get the less approval we get from making mistakes and the more we are judged and judge ourselves. In school, and later at work we get penalized for making mistakes. So over time we internalize this criticism and really start beating ourselves up for our mistakes. The more we beat

ourselves up for our mistakes the more
mistakes we make.

Remember The Law of Attraction says the
more you focus on something the more of
it you get. So if you are focused on your
mistakes you will make more of them. And
the more of them you make, the less you
will like yourself. You will build on your
negative attitude, and stop playing and
laughing because you will think you don't
deserve to have play and laughter in your
life. It all is connected.

Fear of Failure and Success

Fear of failure and fear of success are
the double-edged sword that keep us
from trying new things and hence from
making mistakes. As most of us know fear
of failure is when we don't do things
because we are afraid that we can't do
them or even more important we can't do
them well, or that we might be
embarrassed or make a fool out of
ourselves. Criticism and the thought that
we might have to experience that criticism
keep us from doing many things in life.
Our thought is that if we don't do it we

can't fail at it. I think that by not trying something is the biggest failure there is.

The saddest person I think will be the person on his or her deathbed that thinks I wish I would have done this or done that. The newest brain research indicates that we are never sorry for things we have tried or done, only things that we haven't tried or done. Our brains are wired to learn from every experience, even negative ones. We regret much more what we don't do over what we do.

The fear of success is the opposite of the fear of failure. A person who has fear of success is afraid what will happen to them if they are successful. How might that change their life? Many adults do not like change. The joke is that the only two groups who like change are cashiers and wet babies. Success what might that bring to people? This is what people with fear of success worry about. Does this mean they will have to get new friends? Does this mean they will have to have more successes? Would people's expectations, and more important their own expectations of themselves; would these increase? A person who has these fears rationalizes that not doing something is better than doing something, because they are not sure that they can handle success, or that they even want to. Many times people don't do things because they don't believe that they are deserving of success. Puritan thinking rears its ugly head again; some people think that personal happiness and success are almost down right evil.

Abundance/Scarcity

Related to the fear of making mistakes is the whole issue of abundance and scarcity. Most of us have either an *Abundance Mentality* or a *Scarcity Mentality* of the world. *An Abundance Mentality* perceives the world as being abundant. There is enough for everyone. If I am successful, that does not mean that you can't be. This philosophy says that success breeds success that the universe provides for everyone.

The *Scarcity Mentality,* on the other hand, perceives the world as being scarce. If you have success that means that I won't have it. There is only so much to go around and I had better get mine before you get yours.

With the *Scarcity Mentality*, a person sees the world as very limiting. There are only so many mistakes I can make, I only have limited time, energy, and chances, so I must be very careful with all of them and limit my mistakes.

Someone coming from an *Abundance Mentality* perceives the world very differently. There are an abundance of opportunities. Mistakes are just part of the process. I have plenty of time, resources, energy, and chances.

Susan B. Anthony, I think, had an *Abundance Mentality* because when asked by a reporter when she was in her 80's, if all her work had been in vain to get women the right to vote and other rights, her reply was, "Failure is Impossible!" Now this is a woman who had worked for over 50 years to get women the right to vote, and they hadn't received it yet. Both she and Elizabeth Cady Stanton, who first proposed that women should have the right to vote in 1848, died before women got the right to vote in August 1920.

Thomas Edison probably had an *Abundance Mentality*. When asked by a reporter if he considered all his 10,000 attempts to come up with a light bulb a failure, Edison replied, "I have not failed; I've just found 10,000 ways that won't work. To Edison and other creative people there is a perception that mistakes are part of life and need to be celebrated as such.

The Other Use of YIPPEE

Let's be honest with this one. How many of us look in a mirror and start to feel a little sick or we avoid mirrors all together? This is especially true for me the older I get. Up till 1 year ago when I would look in the mirror I say to myself, "Self, what happened? How did this disaster happen? Did you swallow a waterbed? I mean you look like you are retaining water for the Mormon Tabernacle Choir." It was not a pretty sight. Besides the humor, which was good, I was not doing anything to improve my self-image or positive attitude. The question is how many of you do something like this when you look in the mirror?

Mirror Play

Sadly the Wicked Stepmother in Snow White has given looking in the mirror a bad rap However I have been reading and hearing about *Mirror Work*, (which I call *Mirror Play*), for many years mainly from Louise Hay and others, so I decided about a year ago to put it into action.

This kind of *Mirror Play* can be very beneficial. So each day I go to the mirror naked and I stand back from the mirror and walk up to it with my arms out and once I get about a foot from the mirror I smile at myself in the mirror and say, "YIPPEE! I am alive. I say this with as much enthusiasm as I can muster in the morning. While I am standing there I also look directly into my eyes and say, "Jana, because that's my name, "Jana, I love you exactly as you are." I smile at myself as I am doing this.

At the end of the day I repeat the whole process of "YIPPEE! I am alive, and "Jana, I love you exactly as you are." I don't think we can love ourselves enough or say enough positive things to ourselves. Remember the 12 positives for every 1 negative. If during the day something goes well for me I go to the mirror and say, "Thank You!" If something doesn't go well, again to the mirror I go and say, "That's okay I love you anyway." If we could only learn to love ourselves than maybe we could learn to love others. Thanks go to Louise Hay for teaching me about *Mirror Play*. As Gandhi said, "You must be the change you wish to see in the world." I can't change anyone only myself. I must work on me first.

YIPPEE, reminds you that mistakes are okay and that loving yourself, along with Play, Laughter, Attitude, and Smiles, which I will be talking about, next, can be your Playbook for a healthier and happier life.

Play with These Ideas

o Give yourself permission to make mistakes, lots of mistakes.

o When you make a mistake put your hands above your head and wiggle them and then say, "YIPPEE! How fascinating."

o Realize that life is not a dress rehearsal you need to take risks and not be afraid of failure or success.

o Do *Mirror Play* every day, in the morning and night go to the mirror naked and exclaim with enthusiasm, "YIPPEE, I am alive, and I love myself exactly as I am."

o When things go right for you during the day go to the mirror and say, "Thank You," to yourself.

o When you mess up after you say, "YIPPEE! How fascinating," go to the mirror and say, "That's okay I love you anyway."

Your Page to Play With

PLAY 1

S-SMILE

A smile is a curve that sets everything straight.
Phyllis Diller

Smile is PLAY 1 because if you can't Play, and you can't Laugh, and you can't have a positive Attitude, and you can't say YIPPEE, my hope is that at least you can Smile. Smiling is really the #1 PLAY that we as humans do as babies. It is also the easiest activity of the acronym P.L.A.Y., which is why I have assigned it PLAY 1. Smiling is like laughter, but easier to do and again your brain and your body does not know the difference between a real and a fake smile. There is some interesting research that has been done lately on the benefits of smiling. Kimberly Read in an article called, "What's in a Smile" points out the following:

> In psychology, there is a theory entitled the "facial feedback: hypothesis. This hypothesis states, "Involuntary facial movements provide sufficient peripheral

115

information to drive emotional experience." (Bernstein, et al., 2000) Davis and Palladino explain, "feedback from facial expression affects emotional expression and behavior" (2000). In other words, you may actually be able to improve your mood by simply smiling.

Other studies have found that participants who were instructed to make certain faces experienced autonomic changes similar to those seen with emotions. That is, a person told to make an angry face experienced increased blood flow to the hands and feet, which are also seen in those who are experiencing anger.

Participants from another study involving posed faces reported more favorable impressions of other people when asked to smile. Research has also found that mimicking the face of someone else elicits empathy.

In another research setting, participants were either prevented or encouraged to smile by being instructed how to hold a pencil in their mouths. This experiment found that those who held a pencil in their teeth, and thus were able to smile, rated cartoons as funnier than did those who held the pencil in their lips and thus could not smile.

Paper Straw Smile

This also works with paper straws. I tell my participants to get a straw and bring it with them in their car while driving on the freeway and to put the straw between their teeth, which forces them to smile. By doing this, they feel less upset by stupid drivers who might be on the freeway with them. What makes it even better is to wave at the stupid drivers with the straw in your mouth and your funny smile.

I also challenge the participants in my playshops, as I am challenging you, to go an entire day smiling. This will not be easy, because it turns out that we smile about 1/3 less than we think we do, and men even smile less than women. Women tend to laugh and smile more than men and let out their emotions, which is one reason I think women may live longer than men. Sorry for the aside now back to the challenge. Pick a Monday, since for many people that is the hardest day at work, and attempt to smile all day. If anyone asks you why are smiling and they will, because people think we have to have a reason for smiling and laughing, which we don't have to have a reason. But if anyone asks you why you are smiling just say, as I mentioned before, "I smile because I don't know what the hell is going on around here," and smile some more.

Watch Your Words

So many of us walk around with frowns on our faces, the frown by the way, takes 64 mucscles, while the smile only takes 13, and to make matters worse when asked how we are, we say "FINE." And usually we say FINE, using an extremely low energy tone of voice. So what are we really telling the person who asks us how we are, and even more important, what are we telling ourselves? It has been suggested that when we say FINE, what we really are saying is that we are F...ED-UP, (the bad F word) INSECURE, NEUROTIC, AND EMOTIONAL. I tell people you may want to stop saying you are fine, until you really are FINE.

So what would be some good things to say when asked how you are? Some good things to say are, "I am wonderful! "I am great." Remember the brain and body believes whatever you tell them. My favorite response is, "I am better." Invariably someone says, "Oh I didn't know you had been sick." I answer, "I haven't been, it is just that each and every day I get better and better." That almost always gets a smile if not a laugh from the other person and I really do feel better.

What Does This All Mean?

Well it appears that the next time you are feeling down or blue or just plain old blah-SMILE! Smiling may be the only action that you need to take to improve your spirits. It seems so simple but the positive effects seem more than worthwhile.

Louis Armstrong summed it up best with:

When You're Smiling

When you're smilin'
When you're smilin'
The whole world smiles with you.
And when you're laughin'
When you're laughin'
The sun comes shinin' through.

When you're cryin'
You bring on the rain
So, stop you're sighin'
Won't you be happy again!

When you're smiling
Keep on smilin'
And the whole world smiles with you.

Play with These Ideas

- o Jump on your bed

- o Make funny faces at yourself in the mirror

- o Get a straw and put it in your mouth to force yourself to smile and wave at passing motorists

- o Dance and sing and play

- o Find a playground

- o Find your baby pictures

- o Play with children or pets

- o Hug and kiss someone

- o Take a walk or dance in the rain

- o Watch *Singing in the Rain*, especially the scene with Gene Kelly dancing in the rain

- o Imitate a well-known comedian or politician, many times they are the same person, with exaggeration

Your Page to Play With

PLAY 1550

In The End...

Laugh at yourself first, before anyone else can.
Elsa Maxwell

In the end for me there will be laughter as there was in the beginning. That is how I want it and that is how I am planning it. You know the expression, "I died laughing," I would not mind that at all.

How about you? You know you have a choice in how you view your life. Below is a contract that you can make with yourself to help you live happier and healthier. HAVE FUN!
###############################

My Contract with Myself

I _____, promise to each and every day, play, laugh, have a positive attitude, say YIPPEE every chance I get, and smile at everyone I meet.

Signed_____
Dated_____

Some Great *PLAYS* On Words

- And forget not that the earth delights to feel your bare feet and the winds long to play with your hair. *Kahlil Gibran*

- Be glad of life because it gives you the chance to love and to work and to play and to look up at the stars. *Henry Van Kyke*

- If you aren't playing well, the game isn't as much fun. When that happens I tell myself just to go out and play as I did when I was a kid. *Thomas J. Watson*

- It doesn't matter if you win or lose. It's how you play the game. *Unknown*

- Man is most nearly himself when he achieves the seriousness of a child at play. *Heraclitus*

- The more I want to get something done, the less I call it work. *Richard Bach*

- There is work that is work and there is play that is play: there is play that is work and work that is play. And in only one of these lies happiness. *Gelett Burgess*

- Work and play are words used to describe the same thing under differing conditions. *Mark Twain*

- We don't stop playing because we grow old;
we grow old because we stop playing.
George Bernard Shaw

- The true object of all human life is play.
Earth is a task garden; heaven is a
playground. *K. Chesterton*

- If I had my life to live over...I'd dare to
make more mistakes next time. *Nadine
Stair*

- Whatever you can do, or dream you can,
begin it. Boldness has genius, power, and
magic in it.
Johann Wolfgang von Goethe

- Action seems to follow feeling, but really
action and feeling go together; and by
regulating the action, which is under the
more direct control of the will, we can
indirectly regulate the feeling, which is
not. *William James*

- The universe will reward you for taking
risks on its behalf. *Shakti Gawain*

- Slow down and enjoy life. It's not only the
scenery you miss by going too fast- you
also miss the sense of where you are going
and why. *Eddie Cantor*

- Learn to get in touch with the silence within yourself and know that everything in this life has a purpose.
Elisabeth Kubler-Ross

- Begin to be now what you will be hereafter. *William James*

- Undoubtedly we become what we envisage. *Claude M. Bristol*

- Every time we say Let there be! In any form, something happens. *Stella Terrill Mann*

- Go confidently in the direction of your dreams! Live the life you've imagined. As you simplify your life, the laws of the universe will be simpler. *Henry David Thoreau*

- Belief creates the actual fact. *William James*

- What lies behind us and what lies before us are tiny matters, compared to what lies within us. *Ralph Waldo Emerson*

- What we play is life. *Louis Armstrong*

- At the height of laughter, the universe is flung into a kaleidoscope of new possibilities. *Jean Houston*

- The creative mind plays with the objects its loves. *C.G. Jung*

- We have been taught to believe that negative equals realistic and positive equals unrealistic. *Susan Jeffers*

- I think most of us are as happy as we make up our minds to be. *Abraham Lincoln*
- To live a creative life, we must lose our fear of being wrong. *Joseph Chilton Pearce*

- Affirmations are like prescriptions for certain aspects of yourself you want to change. *Jerry Frankhauser*

- Desire, ask, believe, and receive. *Shella Terrill Mann*

- Genuine beginnings begin within us, even when they are brought to our attention by external opportunities. *William Bridges*

- Take your life in your own hands and what happens? A terrible thing; no one to blame. *Erica Jong*

- Man can alter his life by altering his thinking. *William James*

Books to Play With

1. *Being Happy: A Handbook to Greater Confidence and Security* by Andrew Matthews
2. *Follow Your Heart: Finding Purpose in Your Life and Work* by Andrew Matthews
3. *What the Bleep Do We Know!?: Discovering the Endless Possibilities for Altering Your Everyday Reality* by William Arntz, Betsy Chasse and Mark Vicente, Co-Creators of the Movie: *What the Bleep Do We Know!?* With Jack Forem and Ellen Erwin
4. *As a Man Thinketh* by James Allen
5. *Power vs. Force: The Hidden Determinants of Human Behavior* by David R. Hawkins, M.D., Ph.D.
6. *Adjust You Attitude and Laugh Til the Cows Come Home!* by Linda Henley-Smith
7. *Learned Optimism: How to Change Your Mind and Your Life* by Martin E.P. Seligman, Ph.D.
8. *You Can Heal Your Life* by Louise L. Hay
9. *Comedy Writing Secrets: How to Think Funny, Write Funny, Act Funny and Get Paid for It* by Melvin Helitzer
10. *Improv Wisdom: Don't Prepare, Just Show Up* by Patricia Ryan Madson

11. *Stumbling on Happiness: Think_You Know What Make You Happy?* by Daniel Gilbert

12. *Choosing Joy at Work: Learn the Process of Being Happy and Living More Fully* by Roger Wyer

13. *The Book On Mind Management* by Dennis R. Deaton

14. *Ten Simple Truths that Lead to an Amazing Life: Life is Short Wear Your Party Pants by* Loretta LaRoche

15. *The Artist's Way: A Spiritual Path To Higher Creativity* by Julia Cameron

16. *The Art of Possibility: Transforming Professional and Personal Life* by Rosamund Stone Zander and Benjamin Zander

17. I suggest any books by Dr. Wayne Dyer or Dr. Deepak Chropa

ANOTHER BIGGER WARNING

WARNING: This book is protected by U.S. Copyright Laws, whose enforcement you and I both know mean diddlysquat! There is a better chance of the United States finding WMD's in Iraq, than of a federal marshal or (Jack Bower, from 24) busting you from copying my material. So anyway, nothing in this book may be reproduced, stored in a retrieval system, frozen, shredded, or transmitted in any form or by any means electronic, mechanical, photocopying, recording, paranormal, or otherwise, without the prior notarized written permission of Moi (Yeah, right).